COUNTRY

SOUNDS OF MUSIC

David and Patricia Armentrout

The Rourke Corporation, Inc.
Vero Beach, Florida 32964

PHOTO CREDITS:
© Bruce Carr: cover; © Reuters/Scott Olson/Archive Photos: title page;
© Nashville Banner Publishing Co./Archive Photos: page 4; © Anthony V. Smith:
page 7; © Al Michaud: page 8; © Jeff Greenberg/Intl. Stock: pages 10, 21;
© Reuters/Lee Celano/Archive Photos: page 12; © Reuters/Mike Segar/Archive
Photos: page 13; © Archive Photos: page 15; © Frank Driggs/Archive Photos:
page 17; © Oscar C. Williams: page 18

PRODUCED BY:
East Coast Studios, Merritt Island, Florida

EDITORIAL SERVICES:
Susan Albury

Library of Congress Cataloging-in-Publication Data

Armentrout, David. 1962-
    Country / by David and Patricia Armentrout.
        p. cm. — (Sounds of music)
    Includes bibliographical references (p. 24) and index.
    Summary: Brief text describes different styles of country music, including
bluegrass, cowboy songs, and rockabilly; musical instruments; famous
performers, the recording industry; and country music on television and radio.
    ISBN 0-86593-535-1
    1. Country music—History and criticism Juvenile literature. [1. Country music.]
I. Armentrout, Patricia, 1960- II. Title. III. Series
ML3524.A76 1999
781.642—dc21   99-14251
                                                                          CIP

Printed in the USA

TABLE OF CONTENTS

COUNTRY MUSIC

Country music has been around for a long time, but it was not always called "country." It was first labeled "hillbilly" by the record business. Hillbilly music came from **rural** (RUR ul), or country, areas in the southern United States.

Over the years, different instruments and new **musicians** (myu ZISH enz) changed the sound of hillbilly music. "Country and western" is now the term that describes the popular American musical style.

Trisha Yearwood entertains the crowd at the Country Music Association Awards.

BLUEGRASS

Country and western is a mix of musical styles. One form of country music is bluegrass. Bluegrass music developed from folk and blues styles.

Bluegrass music came from the Ozark and **Appalachian** (ap uh LAY shun) mountain areas. Settlers in these areas sang about everyday life including work, play, love, and death.

Young and old perform a country tune together.

COWBOY SONGS

Another form of country and western developed in the southwest and plains areas. This early style of country music was called "cowboy" music.

Cattle workers sang songs in traditional folk style. Some songs were lullabies. Some songs were stories. Some songs, called **"dogie"** (DOE ghee) songs, helped herd the cattle. Cowboy songs were entertaining and useful.

Music lovers grab a front-row seat at an outdoor jam session.

COUNTRY ON THE RADIO

People from many countries make up the population of the United States. Each group of people brings with them their own musical styles.

How do people share their music? Radio is one way to hear different musical styles.

Just as families today gather to watch television, families in the past gathered to listen to music on the radio. The "Grand Ole Opry" was, and is, a popular radio program that features country music **artists** (ART ests).

Hundreds of thousands tune in weekly to the popular "Grand Ole Opry" radio show.

Shania Twain was awarded "favorite new country artist" at the 1996 American Music Awards.

Garth Brooks regularly tops both the country and pop music charts.

TELEVISION AND MOVIES

At one time country music brought to mind performers wearing bibbed overalls and straw hats. When country music made its way into television and movies, that image changed.

Singers and actors, such as Gene Autry and Roy Rogers, were well known for their western movies and cowboy songs. TV shows like "Hee Haw" combined humor with country music, and brought country-and-western music into millions of homes.

14   *Roy Rogers helped make the singing cowboy image popular.*

COUNTRY VOICES

The country music sound can be heard in the voices of its singers.

The first popular country performers include the Carter Family and Jimmie Rodgers. These artists had two very different singing styles. The Carter Family sang traditional folk-, or mountain-, style music. Jimmie Rodgers had a blues singing style that included **yodels** (YOHD ulz).

Today, country music voices include a mix of blues, folk, and even rock.

Some of the first recorded country music was performed by the Carter Family.

COUNTRY INSTRUMENTS

What do pianos, banjos, fiddles, and electric guitars have in common? They are some of the instruments heard in country music.

Banjos and mandolins bring out the bluegrass sound of country. Fiddles, drums, and saxophones produce a western swing style. Honky tonk, a rural Texas and Oklahoma style, mixes traditional mountain-style singing with the sounds of small electric bands.

An acoustic guitar has either 6 or 12 strings.

COUNTRY ROCKS!

Two terms often describe the combined styles of country and rock and roll. The term *rockabilly* was first used in the 1950s. Most rockabilly performers were rock-and-roll artists who had a country background.

The second term, *country rock,* appeared in the 1970s. Country rock music mixes country **lyrics** (LEER iks), or songs, with instruments common in rock and roll, such as electric guitars.

Country music rocks with the sounds of electric instruments.

A MONEYMAKER

Popular music is written for and sold to large audiences. Popular music is a moneymaker.

What makes country music a moneymaker? It all started with recording companies and the radio. Fans heard the music and bought the records. Recording companies, and the artists, made money from the sales.

Today country music is big business. Money is made from concert tours, music videos, and recording sales.

GLOSSARY

Appalachian (ap uh LAY shun) — a large mountain system in eastern North America that extends from northern Alabama to Quebec

artists (ART ests) — people who create and practice an art such as music writers and performers

dogie (DOE ghee) — a type of song used by cowboys to herd cattle

lyrics (LEER iks) — the words of a song

musician (myu ZISH en) — a writer or performer of music

rural (RUR ul) — country or farming area

yodel (YOHD ul) — a calling singing style where the voice quickly changes from high to low repeatedly

INDEX

FURTHER READING

Find out more about music with these helpful books and information sources:

- *Comprehensive Country Music Encyclopedia.* Editors of Country Music Magazine. Times Books, 1994
- Kingsbury, Paul. *The Grand Ole Opry: History of Country Music.* Villard Books, 1995
- McLin, Lena. *Pulse: A History of Music.* Kjos West, 1977
- Millard, Bob. *Country Music.* HarperCollins, 1993
- "Country and Western Music." Grolier Multimedia Encyclopedia, 1998
- "Country and Western Music." Microsoft Encarta Encyclopedia, 1996